Olivia Petit

Dracula Gegen Manah

Level A2 with Parallel German-English Translation

LANGUAGE
PRACTICE
PUBLISHING

Impressum

Dracula Gegen Manah
by Olivia Petit

Audio tracks and illustrations by Audiolego

Graded German Readers, Volume 23

Homepage www.audiolego.com

Inhaltsverzeichnis
Table of contents

The playback speed

The book is equipped with audio tracks. With the help of QR codes, call up an audio track in no time, without typing a web address manually. VLC Media Player can control the playback speed.

Kapitel 1

Die Reise des Lebens
The Trip of a Lifetime

Es war ein strahlender und sonniger Tag in New York, und die Straßen waren voller Leben. Die Geräusche hupender Autos und das Stimmengewirr der Menschen erfüllten die Luft, als der 10-jährige Tim sich auf den Weg zur Schule machte. Heute war ein wichtiger Tag, denn er würde mehr über seine bevorstehende Klassenfahrt nach Europa erfahren.

Tim war ein neugieriger und abenteuerlustiger Junge, der es liebte, neue Orte und Kulturen kennenzulernen. Er hatte immer davon geträumt, Europa zu besuchen, und jetzt bekam er endlich die Gelegen-

It was a bright and sunny day in New York, and the streets were bustling with life. The sounds of honking cars and the chatter of people filled the air as 10-year-old Tim made his way to school. Today was an important day, as he was going to learn about his upcoming school trip to Europe.

Tim was a curious and adventurous boy who loved to learn about new places and cultures. He had always dreamed of visiting Europe and now, he was finally going to get his chance.

heit dazu.

Als er das Klassenzimmer betrat, begrüßte ihn sein Freund Sam: "Hallo Tim. Es gibt großartige Neuigkeiten über die Klassenfahrt!" Seine Klassenkameraden waren voller Vorfreude und Tim konnte es kaum erwarten, mehr über die Reise zu erfahren.

Ihre Lehrerin, Frau Smith, stand vorne im Raum und wandte sich an die Klasse. "Guten Morgen, Kinder. Ich habe heute aufregende Neuigkeiten für euch. Eure Klasse wird diesen Sommer auf eine Klassenfahrt nach Europa gehen!"

Der Raum brach in Applaus und Jubel aus, und Tims Herz schlug schneller. Er würde nach Europa fahren!

Frau Smith erklärte weiter,

As he entered the classroom, his friend Sam greeted him: "Hi Tim. There is great news about the school trip!" His classmates were all buzzing with anticipation, and Tim couldn't wait to hear more about the trip.

Their teacher, Mrs. Smith, stood at the front of the room and addressed the class. "Good morning, children. I have some exciting news to share with you today. Your class will be going on a school trip to Europe this summer!"

The room erupted in applause and cheers, and Tim's heart skipped a beat. He was going to Europe!

Mrs. Smith went on to

dass die Reise zwei Wochen dauern würde. Sie würden mehrere Länder besuchen, darunter Frankreich, Italien und Rumänien. Sie erwähnte auch, dass sie in Hotels übernachten würden. Es würde viele Möglichkeiten für das Besichtigen von Sehenswürdigkeiten und Abenteuer geben.

Tim war überglücklich. Er war noch nie zuvor mit dem Flugzeug gereist, und jetzt würde er nach Europa reisen und all die erstaunlichen Orte sehen, von denen er nur gelesen hatte.

Im Laufe des Tages konnte Tim nicht aufhören, an die Reise zu denken. Er war so aufgeregt, dass er sich kaum auf den Unterricht konzentrieren konnte. Er konnte es kaum erwarten, seinen Eltern davon zu erzäh-

explain that the trip would last for two weeks. They would be visiting several countries, including France, Italy, and Romania. She also mentioned that they would be staying in hotels. There would be plenty of opportunities for sightseeing and adventure.

Tim was over the moon. He had never been on a plane before, and now he was going to travel to Europe and see all the amazing places he had only read about.

As the day went on, Tim couldn't stop thinking about the trip. He was so excited that he could hardly focus on his lessons. He couldn't wait to tell his par-

len.

Nach der Schule ging Tim mit Sam nach Hause.

"Weißt du, wir werden im Schloss von Graf Dracula in Rumänien übernachten!" sagte Sam.

Tims Augen weiteten sich vor Staunen. "Wirklich? Das ist so cool! Ich kann es kaum erwarten, das Schloss zu erkunden und mehr über seine Geschichte zu erfahren", rief er aus.

Tim eilte nach Hause und stürmte durch die Tür, voller Vorfreude, die Neuigkeiten mit seinen Eltern zu teilen. "Mama, Papa, ihr werdet es nicht glauben! Meine Klasse macht diesen Sommer eine Klassenfahrt nach Europa!"

ents all about it.

After school, Tim walked with Sam home.

"You know, we will stay in Count Dracula's castle in Romania!" Sam said.

Tim's eyes widened in amazement. "Really? That's so cool! I can't wait to explore the castle and learn about its history," he exclaimed.

Tim rushed home and burst through the door, eager to share the news with his parents. "Mom, Dad, you won't believe it! My class is going on a trip to Europe this summer!"

Seine Eltern waren begeistert für ihn und fragten alles über die Reise. Tim erzählte ihnen alles, was er an diesem Tag gelernt hatte. Sie waren beeindruckt von all den erstaunlichen Sehenswürdigkeiten, die er sehen würde.

Die nächsten Wochen vergingen wie im Flug, während Tim und seine Klassenkameraden sich auf ihre Reise vorbereiteten. Sie lernten über die verschiedenen Länder, die sie besuchen würden, und über die verschiedenen Bräuche und Kulturen, denen sie begegnen würden.

Endlich brach der Tag der Reise an. Tim war voller Vorfreude, als er mit seinen Klassenkameraden in das Flugzeug stieg. Als das Flugzeug abhob,

His parents were thrilled for him, and they asked all about the trip. Tim told them everything he had learned that day. They were impressed by all the amazing sights he would get to see.

The next few weeks went by in a blur as Tim and his classmates prepared for their trip. They learned about the different countries they would be visiting and the different customs and cultures they would encounter.

Finally, the day of the trip arrived. Tim was filled with excitement as he boarded the plane with his classmates. As the plane took off, Tim gazed out the

schaute Tim aus dem Fenster und genoss den atemberaubenden Blick auf die Stadt darunter. Er machte sich auf die Reise seines Lebens. Er konnte es kaum erwarten, welche Abenteuer ihn in Europa erwarten würden.

window, taking in the stunning views of the city below. He was going on the trip of a lifetime. He couldn't wait to see what adventures awaited him in Europe.

¿?

Wie war das Wetter am Tag der Ankündigung von Tims Klassenreise?

What was the weather like on the day of Tim's school trip announcement?

Was hat Tim geträumt, bevor die Klassenreise angekündigt wurde?

What did Tim dream of doing before the announcement of the school trip?

Wie hat sich Tim gefühlt, als er von der Klassenreise hörte?

How did Tim feel when he heard the news of the school trip?

Was hat Tims Lehrerin der Klasse mitgeteilt?

What did Tim's teacher announce to the class?

Welche Länder wurden bei der Klassenreise erwähnt?

What countries were mentioned in the school trip?

Wie hat Tim reagiert, als er hörte, dass sie im Schloss von Graf Dracula übernachten würden?

What was Tim's reaction when he heard that they would be staying in Count Dracula's castle?

Wie haben Tims Eltern auf die Nachricht von der Klassenreise reagiert?

How did Tim's parents react to the news of the school trip?

Was haben Tim und seine Klassenkameraden zur Vorbereitung auf die Reise getan?

What did Tim and his classmates do to prepare for the trip?

Wie hat sich Tim gefühlt, als er in das Flugzeug stieg?

How did Tim feel as he boarded the plane?

Was hoffte Tim während seiner Reise nach Europa zu erleben?

What did Tim hope to experience during his trip to Europe?

Audio track

Kapitel 2

Das Abenteuer beginnt
The Adventure Begins

Der Flug nach Frankreich war lang, aber Tim war voller Vorfreude und störte sich nicht an der Zeit. Er verbrachte den gesamten Flug damit, aus dem Fenster zu schauen und die atemberaubende Aussicht von hoch über den Wolken zu genießen.

"Wow, ich kann es kaum glauben, dass wir endlich nach Frankreich fliegen!" sagte Tim zu Sam, der in der Nähe saß.

"Ich freue mich so darauf, den Eiffelturm zu sehen!" antwortete Sam.

"Ich auch! Und all das leckere französische Essen probieren", sagte Tim.

The flight to France was long, but Tim was filled with excitement and didn't mind the time at all. He spent the entire flight looking out the window, taking in the stunning views from high above the clouds.

"Wow, I can't believe we're finally going to France!" Tim said to Sam, who was sitting nearby.

"I'm so excited to see the Eiffel Tower!" Sam answered.

"Me too! And try all the delicious French food," Tim said.

"Ja, Croissants und Baguettes jeden Tag!"

"Haha, ich weiß nicht, ob jeden Tag, aber auf jeden Fall oft!"

Endlich kamen sie in Frankreich an. Tims Herz raste, als er das Flugzeug verließ und seine ersten Schritte in einem fremden Land machte.

Der erste Stopp der Reise war Paris. Tim war fasziniert, als er durch die Straßen der Stadt ging und die Schönheit und Geschichte um ihn herum aufnahm. Sie besuchten den Eiffelturm, das Louvre-Museum und die Kathedrale Notre-Dame. Tim war von der Schönheit jedes einzelnen Ortes beeindruckt.

Die Gruppe unternahm auch eine Bootstour auf der

"Yeah, croissants and baguettes every day!"

"Haha, I don't know about every day, but definitely a lot!"

Finally, they arrived in France. Tim's heart raced as he stepped off the plane and took his first steps in a foreign country.

The first stop on the trip was Paris. Tim was in awe as he walked the streets of the city, taking in the beauty and history that surrounded him. They visited the Eiffel Tower, the Louvre Museum, and the Notre-Dame Cathedral. Tim was amazed by the beauty of each one.

The group also took a boat tour of the Seine River.

Seine. Tim war von den atemberaubenden Ausblicken auf die Stadt vom Wasser aus fasziniert. Er konnte kaum glauben, dass er tatsächlich in Paris war, einer Stadt, die er nur auf Bildern gesehen und in Büchern gelesen hatte.

Nach einigen Tagen in Paris nahm die Gruppe einen Zug nach Italien, wo sie den nächsten Teil der Reise verbringen würden. Tim war aufgeregt, ein neues Land zu sehen und eine andere Kultur zu erleben.

In Italien besuchten sie viele wunderschöne Städte, darunter Rom, Florenz und Venedig. Sie sahen berühmte Wahrzeichen wie das Kolosseum, den Vatikan und die Uffizien. Tim war fasziniert von der reichen

Tim was captivated by the stunning views of the city from the water. He couldn't believe he was actually in Paris, a city he had only ever seen in pictures and read about in books.

After a few days in Paris, the group took a train to Italy, where they would be spending the next part of the trip. Tim was excited to see a new country and to experience a different culture.

In Italy, they visited many beautiful cities, including Rome, Florence, and Venice. They saw famous landmarks like the Colosseum, the Vatican City, and the Uffizi Gallery. Tim was in awe of the rich history

Geschichte und Kunst, die ihn umgab.

"Kannst du glauben, wie schön Italien ist?" sagte er zu Sam.

"Alles ist einfach umwerfend!" antwortete Sam.

"Und das Essen ist unglaublich! Ich könnte jeden Tag Pizza und Pasta essen."

"Mir geht es genauso! Und vergiss das Gelato nicht!"

Einer der Höhepunkte der Reise für Tim war eine Gondelfahrt durch die Kanäle von Venedig. Der Gondoliere sang wunderschöne italienische Lieder, während sie über das Wasser glitten, und Tim war von der Schönheit der Stadt verzaubert.

and art that surrounded him.

"Can you believe how beautiful Italy is?" he said to Sam.

"Everything is just stunning!" Sam answered.

"And the food is amazing! I could eat pizza and pasta every day."

"Same here! And don't forget about gelato!"

One of the highlights of the trip for Tim was a gondola ride through the canals of Venice. The gondolier sang beautiful Italian songs as they glided through the water, and Tim was enchanted by the beauty of the city.

¿?

Wie fühlte sich Tim über den Flug nach Frankreich?

How did Tim feel about the flight to France?

Was war die erste Station der Klassenreise, und welche Sehenswürdigkeiten haben sie dort besucht?

What was the first stop on the school trip, and which landmarks did they visit there?

Wie fühlte sich Tim über die Bootstour auf der Seine?

How did Tim feel about the Seine River boat tour?

Wohin ging die Gruppe nach dem Verlassen von Paris und welche Städte haben sie in diesem Land besucht?

Where did the group go after leaving Paris, and which cities did they visit in that country?

Was war einer der Höhepunkte der Reise für Tim in Italien?

What was one of the highlights of the trip for Tim in Italy?

Kapitel 3

Eine Reise nach Transsilvanien
A Journey to Transylvania

Nach ihren beeindruckenden Erfahrungen in Frankreich und Italien begaben sich Tim und seine Klassenkameraden zu ihrem letzten Ziel: Transsilvanien. Transsilvanien lag im Nordwesten von Rumänien. Sie hatten Gerüchte über ein geheimnisvolles Schloss gehört, das im Herzen der Region liegt, und sie waren gespannt darauf, es zu erkunden.

Als sie in Transsilvanien ankamen, sahen sie die sanften Hügel und dichten Wälder, die das Schloss umgaben. Tim konnte nicht anders, als ein Gefühl von Angst zu verspüren, als sie

After their cool experiences in France and Italy, Tim and his classmates were headed to their final destination: Transylvania. Transylvania was located in the Northwest of Romania. They had heard rumors of a mysterious castle located in the heart of the region, and they were eager to explore it.

When they arrived in Transylvania, they saw the rolling hills and dense forests that surrounded the castle. Tim couldn't help but feel a sense of anxiety

sich dem Schloss näherten. Dann schob er diese Gefühle beiseite und konzentrierte sich auf das Abenteuer, das vor ihnen lag.

Als sie das Schloss betraten, war Tim von seiner Schönheit und Pracht beeindruckt. Die Mauern waren hoch und imposant, und die Hallen waren mit kunstvollen Wandteppichen und Gemälden geschmückt. Aber während sie das Schloss erkundeten, verspürte Tim erneut eine wachsende Angst.

"Wow, dieses Schloss ist wirklich geheimnisvoll!", sagte er zu Sam, der in der Nähe ging.

"Ja, aber es ist auch wirklich cool. Ich kann kaum glauben, dass wir uns an demselben Ort befinden, an dem Dracula gelebt hat."

as they approached the castle. Then he pushed those feelings aside and focused on the adventure that lay ahead.

As they entered the castle, Tim was struck by its beauty and grandeur. The walls were tall and imposing, and the halls were lined with ornate tapestries and paintings. But as they explored the castle, Tim began to feel a growing sense of anxiety again.

"Wow, this castle is really mysterious!" he said to Sam, who was walking nearby.

"Yeah, but it's also really cool. I can't believe we're in the same place where Dracula lived."

"Glaubst du, er ist immer noch hier?", sagte Tim.

"Auf keinen Fall, Dracula war nur eine Figur in einem Buch. Aber es macht Spaß, sich vorzustellen, dass wir sein Schloss erkunden", antwortete Sam.

"Ja, und die Gemälde sind unglaublich. Ich habe das Gefühl, wir sind in einem Märchen."

"Auf jeden Fall. Lass uns weiter erkunden und sehen, welche Geheimnisse dieses Schloss noch birgt. Aber zuerst machen wir ein Foto mit dieser großen Holztür. Lächeln!"

An diesem Punkt erreichten sie den großen Saal, wo sie vom Grafen selbst, Graf Dracula, begrüßt wurden. Tim war überrascht zu sehen, dass der Graf

"Do you think he's still here?" Tim said.

"No way, Dracula was just a character in a book. But it's fun to imagine we're exploring his castle," Sam answered.

"Yeah, and the paintings are amazing. I feel like we're in a fairy tale."

"Definitely. Let's go explore more and see what other secrets this castle holds. But first, let's take a picture with this big wooden door. Smile!"

At this point, they reached the grand hall, where they were greeted by the count himself, Count Dracula. Tim was surprised to see that the

überhaupt nicht dem entsprach, was er erwartet hatte. Er war groß und majestätisch, mit durchdringend kalten blauen Augen und einem charmanten Lächeln. Natürlich war der Mann nur ein Schauspieler...

"Willkommen in meinem Schloss, junge Reisende. Ich bin Graf Dracula", sagte der Graf mit einem Lächeln.

"Äh, hallo, Graf. Ich hätte nicht erwartet, dass Sie so... königlich sind", sagte Frau Smith überrascht.

"Die Leute haben üblicherweise ein bestimmtes Bild von mir im Kopf, aber ich versichere Ihnen, ich bin nur ein Mann", schmunzelte Graf Dracula. "Und es ist mir eine Freude, euch alle in meinem Zuhause willkommen zu heißen", fuhr er mit einem

count was not at all what he had expected. He was tall and regal, with piercing cold blue eyes and a charming smile. Of course, the man was just an actor...

"Welcome to my castle, young travelers. I am Count Dracula," the count said with a smile.

"Uh, hello, Count. I wasn't expecting you to be so... regal," Mrs. Smith said in surprise.

"People tend to have a certain image of me in their minds, but I assure you, I am just a man," Count Dracula chuckled. "And it is a pleasure to have you all here in my home," he continued smiling.

Lächeln fort.

"Vielen Dank, Graf. Wir sind alle sehr aufgeregt, hier zu sein und mehr über die reiche Geschichte Transsilvaniens zu erfahren", antwortete die Lehrerin.

"Ah, ja. Die Geschichte Transsilvaniens ist in der Tat reich, voller Magie und Wunder. Und es wäre mir eine Ehre, euch alles zu zeigen und euch die Geschichten meines Zuhauses zu erzählen", sagte Graf Dracula mit einem erfreuten Ausdruck im Gesicht.

"Das wäre fantastisch, Graf. Wir können es kaum erwarten, mehr zu erfahren", sagte Frau Smith begeistert.

"Sehr gut, dann lasst uns beginnen", sagte Graf Dracula und deutete auf den großen Saal. "Dieser Saal wurde zum Beispiel

"Thank you, Count. We're all very excited to be here and learn more about the rich history of Transylvania," the teacher answered.

"Ah, yes. The history of Transylvania is rich indeed, full of magic and wonder. And I would be honored to show you all around and tell you the stories of my home," Count Dracula said with an expression of pleasure on his face.

"That would be amazing, Count. We all can't wait to learn more," Mrs. Smith said eagerly.

"Very well then, let us begin," Count Dracula said gesturing to the grand hall. "This hall, for example,

einst für große Bälle und Veranstaltungen genutzt. Und diese Gemälde an den Wänden sind Porträts meiner Vorfahren, die große Herrscher Transsilvaniens waren", fuhr er fort und zeigte auf die Wände, an denen riesige Porträts hingen.

"Wow, das ist unglaublich. Ich habe so etwas noch nie gesehen", rief Sam.

"Ich freue mich, dass es dir gefällt, mein Junge", sagte Graf Dracula lächelnd. "Und es gibt noch viel mehr zu sehen. Lasst uns unsere Tour fortsetzen."

was once used for grand balls and events. And these paintings on the walls are portraits of my ancestors, who were great leaders and rulers of Transylvania," he continued pointing to the walls where huge portraits were hanging.

"Wow, this is incredible. I've never seen anything like this before," Sam exclaimed.

"I am glad you like it, my boy," Count Dracula said smiling. "And there is much more to come. Let us continue our tour."

¿?

Wohin waren Tim und seine Klassenkameraden nach ihren Erlebnissen in Frankreich und Italien unterwegs?

Was hörten sie über

Where were Tim and his classmates headed after their experiences in France and Italy?

What did they hear about

Transsilvanien, bevor sie dort ankamen?

Wie fühlte sich Tim, als sie sich dem Schloss näherten?

Was bemerkte Tim, als sie das Schloss betraten?

Über wen sprachen Tim und Sam, als sie das Schloss erkundeten?

Wie reagierte Sam auf Tims Frage nach Draculas Anwesenheit im Schloss?

Wer begrüßte Tim und seine Klassenkameraden in der großen Halle des Schlosses?

Was überraschte Tim an Graf Dracula?

Was sagte Graf Dracula über die Geschichte Transsilvaniens?

Transylvania before arriving there?

How did Tim feel as they approached the castle?

What did Tim notice about the castle as they entered it?

Who did Tim and Sam talk about when they were exploring the castle?

How did Sam respond to Tim's question about Dracula's presence in the castle?

Who greeted Tim and his classmates in the grand hall of the castle?

What surprised Tim about Count Dracula?

What did Count Dracula say about the history of Transylvania?

Was zeigte und erzählte Graf Dracula Tim und seinen Klassenkameraden während der Schlosstour?

What did Count Dracula show and tell Tim and his classmates during the tour of the castle?

Kapitel 4

Ein Zimmer im Nordflügel
A Room in the North Wing

Nach der Tour durch Draculas Schloss kamen Tim und Sam in das Zimmer, das für sie zur Übernachtung reserviert war. Das Zimmer befand sich im Nordflügel des Schlosses.

Tim und Sam schauten sich erstaunt im Raum um. Die Steinwände waren dick und kalt, und die einzige Lichtquelle war eine einzige flackernde Kerze auf dem Nachttisch. Die Möbel waren alt und rustikal, und in den Ecken der Decke hingen Spinnweben.

"Wow, das ist wie aus einem Horrorfilm", sagte Tim und schaute sich im Raum um.

Sam schauderte. "Ich

After the tour through Dracula's castle Tim and Sam came to the room that was reserved for them to stay overnight. The room was in the north wing of the castle.

Tim and Sam looked around the room in amazement. The stone walls were thick and cold, and the only source of light was a single flickering candle on the nightstand. The furniture was old and rustic, and there were cobwebs in the corners of the ceiling.

"Wow, this is like something out of a horror movie," Tim said, looking around the room.

Sam shuddered. "I

weiß, ich habe Gänsehaut. Glaubst du, es gibt wirklich Geister in diesem Schloss?"

"Ich weiß es nicht", sagte Tim, "aber ich habe gehört, dass Graf Dracula selbst diese Gänge heimsucht."

Sam schluckte, versuchte aber zu lächeln. "Ich hoffe, er kommt heute Nacht nicht zu Besuch."

Plötzlich hörten sie ein lautes Klopfen an der Tür.

"Wer könnte das sein?", sagte Tim.

Sam ging zur Tür und öffnete sie. Dort stand im Flur Mrs. Smith.

"Hallo, Jungs", sagte sie mit einem Lächeln. "Ich wollte nur nach euch sehen und sicherstellen, dass ihr euch gut

know, it's giving me the creeps. Do you think there are really ghosts in this castle?"

"I don't know," Tim said, "but I heard that Count Dracula himself haunts these halls."

Sam gulped but tried to smile. "I hope he doesn't come visit us tonight."

Suddenly, there was a loud knock at the door.

"Who could that be?" Tim said.

Sam walked to the door and opened it. There, standing in the hallway, was Mrs. Smith.

"Hello, boys," she said with a smile. "I just wanted to check on you and make

eingelebt habt."

Tim und Sam atmeten erleichtert auf. "Uns geht es gut, Frau Smith", sagte Tim. "Wir sind nur ein wenig verängstigt von der Tour."

Frau Smith lachte. "Ich kann es mir vorstellen. Dieses Schloss kann einem das Gefühl geben, dass es ein Teil von einem ist. Aber keine Sorge, es ist alles nur zum Spaß."

Sie sagte auch, dass die anderen Kinder aus ihrer Gruppe Zimmer in anderen Teilen des Schlosses bekamen. Frau Smith bekam ein Zimmer im Blutigen Turm, der in der Nähe der alten Steinbrücke lag.

"Wir werden jetzt das nahegelegene Dorf besuchen, um auf dem Markt der Einheimischen Souvenirs zu kaufen",

sure you're settling in okay."

Tim and Sam breathed a sigh of relief. "We're fine, Mrs. Smith," Tim said. "Just a little spooked from the tour."

Mrs. Smith chuckled. "I can imagine. This castle can make you feel like it's a part of you. But don't worry, it's all just for fun."

She also said that other children from their group got rooms in other parts of the castle. Mrs. Smith got a room in the Bloody Tower that was located near the ancient stone bridge.

"We are going to visit the nearby village now to buy some souvenirs at the local people's market," Mrs.

fuhr Frau Smith fort. "Der Bus fährt in zehn Minuten ab."

Nach einigen Minuten stiegen die Kinder und die Lehrerin in den Bus ein und der Bus fuhr los in Richtung des Dorfes. Die Straße führte durch einen Wald. Die Bäume auf beiden Seiten der Straße waren hoch und imposant und warfen lange Schatten über das Gras. Die Sonne ging unter und malte den Himmel in Schattierungen von Rot und Orange, die sich vom dunklen Grün des Waldes abhoben. Manchmal, wenn der Bus durch einen dichten Wald fuhr, war es sehr dunkel. Aber wenn die Straße durch Wiesen führte, sah der rote Himmel wie ein riesiges Zelt aus, das über den Bergen aufgespannt war. Manchmal schien der schwarze Wald die

Smith continued. "The bus is leaving in ten minutes."

In several minutes the children and the teacher got on the bus and the bus started for the village. The road went through a forest. The trees on either side of the road were tall and imposing, casting long shadows across the grass. The sun was setting down, painting the sky with shades of red and orange, which contrasted with the dark green of the forest. Sometimes, when the bus was going through a thick forest, it was very dark. But when the road went through meadows, the red sky above looked like a huge tent that was put over the mountains. Sometimes the black forest

Straße zu umschließen und drohte jeden zu verschlingen, der es wagte, zu weit zu gehen. Aber trotz der dunklen Bäume hatte die Straße eine geheimnisvolle Schönheit. Die letzten Strahlen der untergehenden Sonne tanzten durch die Bäume und warfen flackernde Schatten auf die Straße. Die Luft war kühl und erfrischend.

seemed to be closing in around the road, threatening to swallow up anyone who dared to go too far. But despite the dark trees, the road had a haunting beauty. The last rays of the setting sun danced through the trees, casting flickering shadows across the road. The air was cool and refreshing.

¿?

Wo befand sich das Zimmer für Tim und Sam?

Where was the room for Tim and Sam located?

Woher kam das Licht im Zimmer?

What was the source of light in the room?

Wie war der Zustand der Möbel im Zimmer?

What was the condition of the furniture in the room?

Wen hörte Tim, dass die Gänge des Schlosses heimsucht?

Who did Tim hear haunts the halls of the castle?

Wo bekam Frau Smith ein

Where did Mrs. Smith

Zimmer im Schloss?

Wohin wollten die Kinder einen Besuch abstatten?

Wie würdest du die Schönheit der Straße beschreiben?

get a room in the castle?

Where were the children going to visit?

How would you describe the road's beauty?

Kapitel 5

Das Treffen mit Manah
The Meeting with Manah

Der Markt befand sich auf dem Dorfplatz, der nur vom roten Abendhimmel beleuchtet wurde. Es gab Reihen von Ständen, die traditionelle rumänische Souvenirs verkauften, wie zum Beispiel Holzspielzeug, handgeschnitzte Figuren und bestickte Kleidung. Es gab auch Stände, die lokal hergestellten Honig, Wein und Käse verkauften. Der Duft von frisch gebackenem Brot zog durch die Luft und verlockte hungrige Kunden, anzuhalten und die Waren zu probieren.

Mit zunehmender Abenddämmerung wurde der Markt

The market was in the village square, which was only lit up with the red evening sky. There were rows of stalls selling traditional Romanian souvenirs, such as wooden toys, hand-carved figurines, and embroidered clothing. There were also stalls selling locally made honey, wine, and cheeses. The smell of freshly baked bread wafted through the air, tempting hungry shoppers to stop and sample the wares.

As the evening wore

noch lebendiger. Musiker begannen traditionelle rumänische Musik zu spielen und die Menschen versammelten sich, um zu tanzen und zu singen. Die Atmosphäre war festlich und fröhlich, und Menschen jeden Alters genossen den warmen Sommerabend.

Der Markt war auch ein großartiger Ort, um einzigartige Souvenirs im Zusammenhang mit Graf Dracula zu kaufen. Es gab Stände, die Miniatur-Repliken des Schlosses verkauften, sowie T-Shirts, Tassen und Schlüsselanhänger mit Vampir-Motiven. Für diejenigen, die abenteuerlustiger waren, gab es sogar Stände, die Knoblauchknollen und Silberschmuck verkauften, die angeblich vor Vampiren schützen.

on, the market became even more lively. Musicians began to play traditional Romanian music, and people gathered around to dance and sing. The atmosphere was festive and joyful, with people of all ages enjoying the warm summer evening.

The market was also a great place to buy unique souvenirs related to Count Dracula. There were stalls selling miniature replicas of the castle, along with vampire-themed T-shirts, mugs, and keychains. For those feeling more adventurous, there were even stalls selling garlic bulbs and silver jewelry, said to protect against vampires.

"Wow, schau dir all diese Souvenirs an. Die sind so cool!" sagte Sam.

"Ich weiß! Hey, was ist das für eine Holzpuppe da drüben?" fragte Tim.

"Ah, das ist Manah. Er ist etwas Besonderes", antwortete der Verkäufer.

"Was ist so besonders an ihm?"

"Nun, Manah wurde von Geppetto gemacht, demselben Mann, der Pinocchio gemacht hat. Geppetto besuchte dieses Dorf vor ungefähr zweihundert Jahren und machte diese Puppe für meinen Vorfahren, um ihn und seine Familie zu beschützen", fuhr der Verkäufer fort.

Manah war eine Holzpuppe mit einem blassen, glatten Gesicht und tiefen schwarzen Au-

"Wow, look at all of these souvenirs. They're so cool!" Sam said.

"I know! Hey, what's that wooden doll over there?" Tim asked.

"Ah, you're looking at Manah. He's quite special," the seller answered.

"What's so special about him?"

"Well, Manah was made by Geppetto, the same man who made Pinocchio. Geppetto visited this village about two hundred years ago and made this doll for my ancestor to protect him and his family," the seller continued.

Manah was a wooden doll with a pale, smooth face and deep black eyes.

gen. Sein Haar bestand aus dünnen, feinen Holzsträhnen, die zu einem kurzen Bob gestylt waren. Er trug ein einfaches Kleid aus weichem Stoff, das sich über sein hölzernes Gestell drapierte.

"Was Manah von anderen Puppen unterscheidet, ist seine unglaubliche Fähigkeit, gegen dunkle Mächte zu schützen. Wenn Gefahr naht, werden seine langen Arme noch weiter ausgestreckt und länger und flexibler, als man es für möglich halten würde für eine Holzpuppe. Dadurch kann er diejenigen einfangen und festhalten, die seinem Herrn Schaden zufügen wollen. Viele glauben, dass diese außergewöhnliche Fähigkeit vom Holz kommt, das zur Erschaffung von Manah verwendet wurde. Geppetto wählte sorgfältig eine besondere Art von Holz

His hair was made of thin, delicate strands of wood that were styled into a short bob. He wore a simple dress made of soft fabric that draped over his wooden frame.

"What sets Manah apart from other dolls is his incredible ability to protect against dark powers. When danger is near, his long arms will stretch out even further, becoming longer and more flexible than one would think is possible for a wooden doll. This allows him to catch and hold those who are going to harm his master. Many believe that this extraordinary ability comes from the wood used to create Manah. Geppetto carefully selected a special

aus, das mit schützender Magie durchdrungen war", fügte der Verkäufer hinzu.

Ob es sein durchdringender Blick oder seine übernatürlichen Fähigkeiten waren, Manah war eine wirklich bemerkenswerte Puppe.

"Kann ich ihn kaufen?" fragte Tim.

"Ich fürchte, ich kann Manah nicht verkaufen. Er ist mir zu wertvoll und sentimental", antwortete der Verkäufer. "Bitte wählen Sie eines der Souvenirs an meinem Stand und ich werde mich freuen, es zu verkaufen."

"Ich habe eine neue und teure Kamera. Ich wäre bereit, sie gegen Manah einzutauschen", bot Tim an und zeigte dem Verkäufer die Kamera.

type of wood, one that was infused with protective magic," the seller added.

Whether it was his piercing gaze or his otherworldly abilities, Manah was a truly remarkable doll.

"Can I buy him?" Tim asked.

"I'm afraid I cannot sell Manah. He's too valuable and sentimental to me," the seller answered. "Please, choose any of the souvenirs in my stall and I will be happy to sell them."

"I have a new and expensive camera. I would be willing to trade it for Manah," Tim offered and showed the camera to the seller.

"Hmm, das ist ein verlockendes Angebot. Lassen Sie mich einen Moment darüber nachdenken", antwortete der Verkäufer und betrachtete die Kamera sorgfältig. Nach einem Moment des Nachdenkens nickte der Verkäufer mit dem Kopf.

"In Ordnung, ich tausche Manah gegen Ihre Kamera.

Aber denken Sie daran, Manah ist..."

Plötzlich war ein lautes Heulen zu hören. Zuerst war es fern und leise, aber als es lauter wurde, begannen die Menschen aufmerksam zu werden. Das Heulen des Wolfs hallte durch den Wald, prallte von den Bäumen und Hügeln ab und drang bis zum Markt im Dorf vor. Die Musiker hörten auf, Musik zu spielen. Mütter hielten ihre kleinen Kin-

"Hmm, that's quite an offer. Let me think about it for a moment," the seller answered looking carefully at the camera. After a moment of thought, the seller nodded his head.

"Alright, I'll trade you Manah for your camera.

But remember, Manah is..."

Suddenly a loud howling was heard. At first, it was distant and faint, but as it grew louder, the people began to take notice. The howling of the wolf echoed through the forest, bouncing off the trees and hills, and carried all the way to the market in the village. Musicians stopped playing music. Mothers

der eng an sich und machten sich auf den Weg nach Hause, während die Verkäufer begannen, ihre Stände zu schließen, ihre Waren zu verpacken und den Markt zu verlassen. Nach einer Minute war fast niemand mehr dort.

clutched their little children close and began making their way towards home, while the sellers started to close their stalls, packing up their goods and leaving the market. In a minute there was almost nobody left there.

¿?

Welche traditionellen rumänischen Souvenirs wurden auf dem Markt verkauft?

What traditional Romanian souvenirs were being sold at the market?

Welche Arten von Lebensmitteln wurden auf dem Markt verkauft?

What types of food were being sold at the market?

Wie war die Atmosphäre auf dem Markt?

What was the atmosphere like at the market?

Welche einzigartigen Souvenirs im Zusammenhang mit Graf Dracula wurden auf dem Markt verkauft?

What unique souvenirs related to Count Dracula were being sold at the market?

Wer hat die Holzpuppe namens Manah hergestellt?

Was macht Manah zu einer besonderen Puppe?

Warum hat der Verkäufer sich zuerst geweigert, Manah zu verkaufen?

Was hat Tim angeboten, um Manah zu tauschen?

Was passierte, als das Heulen eines Wolfs zu hören war?

Who made the wooden doll named Manah?

What makes Manah a special doll?

Why did the seller refuse to sell Manah at first?

What did Tim offer to trade for Manah?

What happened when the howling of a wolf was heard?

Kapitel 6

Die Gute-Nacht-Geschichte von Graf Dracula

Count Dracula's Bedtime Story

Tim und Sam lagen beide in ihren Betten, hellwach in dem schwach beleuchteten Raum von Graf Draculas Schloss.

"Sam, hörst du das?" fragte Tim.

"Was?"

"Jemand klopft an die Tür", sagte Tim.

Sam setzte sich im Bett auf und hörte aufmerksam hin. Auch er konnte das leise Klopfen hören, das von draußen an ihrer Schlafzimmertür erklang. Die Jungs stiegen aus dem Bett und näherten sich der Tür. Tim öffnete sie, und beide blickten in

Tim and Sam were both lying in their beds, wide awake in the dimly lit room of Count Dracula's castle.

"Sam, do you hear that?" Tim asked.

"What?"

"Someone's knocking on the door," Tim said.

Sam sat up in bed and listened carefully. He too could hear the faint sound of knocking coming from outside their bedroom door. The boys got out of bed and approached the door. Tim opened it, and they both looked out into

den Flur. Sie sahen eine Gestalt im Schatten stehen, und als sie näher kam, erkannten sie, dass es Graf Dracula war.

"Guten Abend", sagte Graf Dracula.

"Guten Abend, Graf Dracula", antworteten Tim und Sam im Chor.

"Ich entschuldige mich für die Störung. Darf ich hereinkommen?"

"Ja, bitte", antworteten sie.

Graf Dracula betrat den Raum, in dem Tim und Sam sich auf das Zubettgehen vorbereiteten.

"Heute Abend habe ich eine besondere Gutenachtgeschichte für euch", sagte der Graf und deutete auf die Stühle. "Setzt euch und hört zu."

the hallway. They saw a figure standing in the shadows, and as it got closer, they realized that it was Count Dracula.

"Good evening," Count Dracula said.

"Good evening, Count Dracula," Tim and Sam replied in unison.

"I apologize for the disturbance. May I come in?"

"Yes, please,"

Count Dracula entered the room where Tim and Sam were getting ready for bed.

"Tonight, I have a special bedtime story for you," the count said, gesturing to chairs. "Sit down and listen."

Die Jungs schauten sich an und setzten sich auf die Stühle.

"Es war einmal ein Wissenschaftler namens Griffin, der einen Weg entdeckte, unsichtbar zu werden. Zuerst dachte er, es wäre ein Segen. Doch bald merkte er, dass Unsichtbarkeit auch ihre Nachteile hatte", begann der Graf.

Die Jungs lauschten gespannt, während der Graf seine Geschichte vom unsichtbaren Mann erzählte und beschrieb, wie Griffin seine neu gewonnenen Kräfte sowohl für Gutes als auch für Böses einsetzte.

"Er konnte sich unbemerkt herumschleichen. Aber seine Unsichtbarkeit machte ihn auch zu einem Außenseiter", fuhr der Graf fort. "Griffin begann den Bezug zur Realität zu verlieren."

The boys looked at each other and sat down on the chairs.

"Once upon a time, there was a scientist named Griffin who discovered a way to become invisible. At first, he thought it would be a blessing. However soon he realized that being invisible had its downsides," the count began.

The boys listened intently as the count weaved his tale of the invisible man, describing how Griffin used his newfound powers for both good and evil.

"He was able to sneak around undetected. But his invisibility also made him an outcast," the count continued. "Griffin began to lose touch with reality."

Die Jungs waren fasziniert von der Geschichte und warteten gespannt auf das Ende.

"Der Höhepunkt der Geschichte kam, als Griffins Rachepläne zu weit gingen und er zum gesuchten Verbrecher wurde. Er erkannte, dass seine Unsichtbarkeit ihn verwundbarer gemacht hatte als je zuvor", fasste der Graf zusammen.

Die Jungs waren beide von der Geschichte des unsichtbaren Mannes gefesselt. Sie saßen einen Moment lang schweigend da und nahmen alles in sich auf.

"Dankeschön, Graf Dracula", meldete sich Sam schließlich zu Wort. "Das war eine erstaunliche Geschichte."

"Ja, vielen Dank", fügte Tim gähnend hinzu.

"Gern geschehen, Jungs",

The boys were fascinated by the story and eagerly waited to hear how it ended.

"The climax of the story happened when Griffin's plans for revenge went too far, and he became a wanted criminal. He realized that his invisibility had made him more vulnerable than ever before," the count concluded.

The boys were both spellbound by the tale of the invisible man. They sat in silence for a few moments, taking it all in.

"Thank you, Count Dracula," Sam finally spoke up. "That was an amazing story."

"Yes, thank you," Tim added with a yawn.

"You're welcome,

sagte der Graf mit einem Lächeln. "Jetzt ist es Zeit, dass ihr schlafen geht."

Während Graf Dracula sich darauf vorbereitete, das Zimmer der Jungs zu verlassen, drehte er sich zu ihnen um und sprach mit ernster Stimme:

"Jetzt, Jungs, muss ich euch warnen, dass in diesem Schloss viele dunkle Kräfte am Werk sind.

Aber ich hoffe, dass euch die Geschichte, die ich heute Abend mit euch geteilt habe, gelehrt hat, dass mit großer Macht große Verantwortung einhergeht."

Tim und Sam nickten und versuchten die Warnung des Grafen zu verstehen.

boys," the count said with a smile. "Now, it's time for you to get some sleep."

As Count Dracula prepared to leave the boys' room, he turned to them and spoke in a serious tone,

"Now, boys, I must warn you that there are many dark powers at play in this castle.

But I hope that the tale I shared with you tonight has taught you that with great power comes great responsibility."

Tim and Sam nodded, trying to understand the count's warning.

"Ich wünsche euch beiden einen friedlichen und ungestörten Schlaf", sagte Graf Dracula, während er auf die Tür zusteuerte.

"Dankeschön, Graf Dracula", sagten die Jungs im Chor.

Der Graf hielt inne und drehte sich wieder zu ihnen um. "Denkt daran, wenn ihr euch jemals in diesem Schloss fürchtet, zögert nicht, mich zu suchen."

Die Jungs lächelten und waren dankbar für das Hilfsangebot des Grafen.

"Gute Nacht, Jungs", sagte Graf Dracula mit einem Lächeln und verließ dann den Raum.

Als sich die Tür schloss, fühlten Tim und Sam sich beruhigt, denn sie wussten, dass sie sich an Graf Dracula wenden

"I wish you both a peaceful and undisturbed sleep," Count Dracula said as he headed towards the door.

"Thank you, Count Dracula," the boys said in unison.

The count paused and turned back towards them. "Remember, if you ever feel afraid in this castle, don't hesitate to come find me."

The boys smiled, grateful for the count's offer of help.

"Good night, boys," Count Dracula said with a smile, and then he left the room.

As the door closed, Tim and Sam felt a sense of comfort knowing that they had

konnten, wenn sie jemals Hilfe brauchten.

Als sie sich in ihre Betten legten, heulte der Wind draußen und die Kerze flackerte. Tim und Sam versuchten, das Knarren der Dielen und die raschelnden Geräusche in den Wänden zu ignorieren, aber sie konnten nicht anders, als das Gefühl zu haben, beobachtet zu werden.

Gerade als sie kurz davor waren, einzuschlafen, hörten sie ein seltsames Geräusch, das vom Fenster kam. Sie schauten hinüber und sahen ein Paar leuchtende Augen, die ihnen zurückstarrten.

Sie schrien und kauerten sich ängstlich unter die Decken, zu verängstigt, um sich zu bewegen. Doch während sie in

Count Dracula to turn to if they ever needed help.

As they settled into their beds, the wind howled outside and the candle flickered. Tim and Sam tried to ignore the creaking floorboards and the rustling sounds in the walls, but they couldn't help feeling like they were being watched.

Just as they were about to drift off to sleep, they heard a strange noise coming from the window. They looked over and saw a pair of glowing eyes staring back at them.

They screamed and huddled together under the covers, too scared to move. But as they waited in terror,

Angst warteten, erkannten sie, dass die Augen zu nichts anderem gehörten als einer freundlichen Fledermaus, die durch das offene Fenster hereingeflogen war.

Erleichtert lachten Tim und Sam über sich selbst, dass sie so erschrocken waren. Sie schlossen ihre Augen und schliefen ein, in der Hoffnung, dass die dunklen Kräfte des Schlosses ihren friedlichen Schlaf nicht stören würden. Sie schliefen ein, während die Fledermaus im Raum herumflog und froh waren, eine Nacht im berühmt-berüchtigten Schloss des Grafen Dracula zu verbringen.

they realized that the eyes belonged to nothing more than a friendly bat, who had flown in through the open window.

Relieved, Tim and Sam laughed at themselves for being so scared. They closed their eyes and drifted off to sleep, hoping that the dark powers of the castle would not disturb their peaceful slumber. They fell asleep with the bat flying around the room, happy to be spending a night in the infamous Count Dracula's castle.

¿?

Wer klopfte an die Tür vor dem Schlafzimmer der Jungen?

Who was knocking on the door outside the boys' bedroom?

Welche besondere Gute-Nacht-Geschichte erzählte Graf Dracula den Jungen?

Was ist in der Geschichte mit Griffin passiert?

Welche Warnung gab Graf Dracula den Jungen, bevor er ihr Zimmer verließ?

Was haben Tim und Sam draußen vor ihrem Fenster gesehen, das sie erschreckt hat?

Wie fühlten sich Tim und Sam, als sie einschliefen?

What special bedtime story did Count Dracula tell the boys?

What happened to Griffin in the story?

What warning did Count Dracula give to the boys before he left their room?

What did Tim and Sam see outside their window that scared them?

How did Tim and Sam feel as they went to sleep?

Kapitel 7

Tim sucht nach Sam
Tim Is Searching for Sam

Tim's Augen öffneten sich im Dunkeln, der Mond warf einen schwachen Schein durch das Fenster des alten Schlosses. Er setzte sich im Bett auf, das Geräusch seines eigenen Atems hallte in seinen Ohren wider. Etwas stimmte nicht.

Tim warf einen Blick auf das Bett neben sich und sah, dass es leer war. Panik ergriff sein Herz, als er sich daran erinnerte, dass Sam, sein Freund, dort nur wenige Stunden zuvor geschlafen hatte.

"Sam?" flüsterte er, seine

Tim's eyes flickered open in the darkness, the moon casting a dim glow through the window of the old castle. He sat up in bed, the sound of his own breathing echoing in his ears. Something was not right.

Tim glanced over to the bed beside him and saw that it was empty. Panic gripped his heart as he remembered that Sam, his friend, had been sleeping there just a few hours ago.

"Sam?" he whispered,

Stimme kaum hörbar in dem stillen Raum. Keine Antwort.

Tim schwang die Beine aus dem Bett, der kalte Steinboden schickte Schauer über seinen Rücken. Er stand auf, seine Augen gewöhnten sich an das schwache Licht. Er wusste, dass er Sam finden musste.

Als er sich leise zur Tür schlich, hörte er ein leises Geräusch, wie ein Wimmern. Er erstarrte und lauschte angestrengt. Es kam aus dem Flur draußen. Er holte tief Luft und trat in den Korridor.

Das Schloss war still, das einzige Geräusch das Echo seiner Schritte, während er über den kalten Steinboden ging. Noch nie hatte er sich so allein und verwundbar gefühlt. Das Einzige, woran er dachte, war,

his voice barely audible in the silent room. No answer came.

Tim swung his legs out of bed, the cold stone floor sending shivers up his spine. He stood up, his eyes adjusting to the dim light. He knew he had to find Sam.

As he tiptoed towards the door, he heard a faint sound, like a whimper. He froze, straining his ears. It came from the hallway outside. He took a deep breath and stepped into the corridor.

The castle was silent, the only sound the echo of his footsteps as he moved along the cold stone floor. He had never felt so alone and vulnerable in his life. The only thing on his mind

Sam zu finden.

Als er um eine Ecke bog, sah er ein schwaches Licht in der Ferne. Er beschleunigte seine Schritte, in der Hoffnung, dass es Sam war. Das Licht wurde heller, und er konnte sehen, dass es von einem Raum am Ende des Korridors kam.

Er öffnete die Tür und trat ein. Der Raum war leer, aber das Licht kam von einer Kerze auf dem Tisch. Sam war nirgendwo zu sehen.

Tims Herz sank, als er feststellte, dass er immer noch allein war. Er durchsuchte den Raum hektisch, rief Sams Namen, aber es kam keine Antwort. Er wollte gehen, als er etwas Seltsames an der Kerze bemerkte. Sie brannte immer noch, aber das Wachs war her-

was finding Sam.

As he turned a corner, he saw a faint light up ahead. He quickened his pace, hoping that it was Sam. The light grew brighter, and he could see that it was coming from a room at the end of the corridor.

He pushed the door open and stepped inside. The room was empty, but the light was coming from a candle on the table. Sam was nowhere to be seen.

Tim's heart sank as he realized that he was still alone. He searched the room frantically, calling out Sam's name, but there was no answer. He was about to leave when he noticed something strange about the candle. It was still burn-

untergeschmolzen und enthüllte eine in das Holz des Tisches eingravierte Botschaft.

"Folge der Spur",

stand dort.

Tims Herz setzte einen Schlag aus. Welche Spur? Er schaute sich im Raum um, aber da war nichts zu sehen. Dann bemerkte er eine schwache Linie auf dem Boden, die aus dem Raum herausführte. Sie war fast unsichtbar, aber im Kerzenlicht konnte er sie gerade noch erkennen.

Er folgte der Linie, sein Herz raste. Sie führte ihn durch dunkle, verwinkelte Korridore und Treppen. Er hatte das Gefühl, in einem Labyrinth zu sein, das Schloss schien sich um ihn herum zu verschieben und

ing, but the wax had melted down to reveal a message etched into the wood of the table.

"Follow the trail," it read.

Tim's heart skipped a beat. What trail? He looked around the room, but there was nothing to be seen. Then he noticed a faint line on the floor, leading out of the room. It was almost invisible, but he could just make it out in the candlelight.

He followed the line, his heart racing. It led him through dark, winding corridors and up and down staircases. He felt as though he were in a maze, the castle seeming to shift and

verändern.

Schließlich gelangte er zu einer Tür am Ende eines langen Flurs. Die Linie führte direkt hindurch. Tim wollte die Tür öffnen, hörte jedoch Stimmen dahinter. Er schaute durch einen Spalt in der Tür. Er bemerkte Dracula, der in der großen Halle des Schlosses stand und seinen durchdringenden Blick über die Gästeschar schweifen ließ.

"Willkommen, meine lieben Freunde", rief er aus, seine Stimme hallte durch die Halle. "Es lässt mein Herz gefrieren, eine solche Versammlung von Legenden und Albträumen zu sehen."

change around him.

Finally, he came to a door at the end of a long hallway. The line led straight through it. Tim wanted to open the door, but then he heard some voices behind it. He looked into a crack in the door. He noticed Dracula, who stood in the grand hall of the castle, his piercing gaze scanning the crowd of guests that filled the hall.

"Welcome, my dear friends," he called out, his voice echoing through the hall. "It freezes my heart to see such a gathering of legends and nightmares."

Die Mumie schlich vor, ihre Bandagen raschelten, als sie sprach. "Wir würden es für nichts auf der Welt verpassen, Graf Dracula. Es ist eine Ehre, zu Ihrer Geburtsnachtsfeier eingeladen zu sein."

Der Wolfsmensch ließ ein tiefes Knurren hören, als er voranschritt. "Ich stimme zu. Wir mögen Kreaturen der Nacht sein, aber auch wir wissen, wie man feiert."

Der unsichtbare Mann lachte, seine Stimme schien aus dem Nichts zu kommen. "Ich versichere Ihnen, Graf Dracula, dass wir alle gekommen sind, um Spaß zu haben."

Freddy Krueger neigte seinen Hut nach vorne, seine scharfen Krallen glänzten im Kerzenlicht. "Und vielleicht ein

The Mummy stepped forward, his bandages rustling as he spoke. "We wouldn't miss it for the world, Count Dracula. It's an honor to be invited to your birthnight celebration."

The Wolf Man let out a low growl as he stepped forward. "I agree. We may be creatures of the night, but even we know how to party."

The Invisible Man chuckled, his voice seeming to come from nowhere. "I can assure you, Count Dracula, that we have all come to have a good time."

Freddy Krueger tilted his hat forward, his sharp claws glinting in the candle-

bisschen Unfug treiben", fügte er mit einem verschmitzten Grinsen hinzu.

Chucky, die Puppe, kicherte, während sie vorwackelte. "Ich will einfach nur tanzen!" rief Chucky aus, seine kleinen Beine hüpften auf und ab.

Dracula lachte, seine Augen strahlten vor Vergnügen. "Dann lasst uns tanzen und bis zum Morgengrauen feiern", verkündete er und streckte seine Arme einladend aus.

Warum ist Tim aus dem Bett gestiegen?

Was hat Tim im Flur gehört?

Was hat Tim am Ende des Flurs gesehen?

---

light. "And maybe cause a little mischief," he added with a sly grin.

Chucky, the doll, cackled as he waddled forward. "I just want to dance!" he exclaimed, his little legs bouncing up and down.

Dracula laughed, his eyes alight with amusement. "Then let's dance and feast until the dawn," he declared, raising his arms in welcome.

Why did Tim get out of bed?

What did Tim hear in the hallway?

What did Tim see at the end of the corridor?

Was hat die Botschaft auf dem Tisch Tim gesagt, dass er tun soll?

Was hat Tim am Ende der Linie auf dem Boden gefunden?

Was hat Tim gesehen, als er in den Spalt der Tür geschaut hat?

Wer waren die Gäste im großen Saal des Schlosses?

What did the message on the table tell Tim to do?

What did Tim find at the end of the line on the floor?

What did Tim see when he looked into the crack in the door?

Who were the guests in the grand hall of the castle?

Kapitel 8

Graf Draculas Geburtsnacht
Count Dracula's Birthnight

Die Gäste umgaben Dracula und Sam, ihre leeren Gläser gierig ausgestreckt, während sie hungrig zusahen. Dracula selbst hatte Sam auf einem Fass in der Mitte des Raumes platziert, ein böses Grinsen auf dem Gesicht, während er auf seine Gäste deutete.

Sam fröstelte vor Angst, seine Augen wanderten ängstlich im Raum umher, während er versuchte, einen Fluchtweg zu finden. Doch es gab keine Hoffnung – die Gäste hatten ihn umzingelt, und Dracula selbst stand Wache.

„Frohe Geburtsnacht, Dracula!"

Dracula's guests had surrounded him and Sam, their empty glasses held out eagerly as they looked on hungrily. Dracula himself had placed Sam on a barrel in the center of the room, a wicked grin on his face as he gestured to his guests.

Sam shivered in fear, his eyes darting around the room as he tried to find a way to escape. But there was no hope—the guests had surrounded him, and Dracula himself stood guard.

"Happy birthnight, Dracula!"

riefen die Gäste im Chor, ihre Stimmen hallten durch den Raum.

Dracula grinste breit, seine Zähne glänzten im schwachen Licht. „Danke, meine Freunde", sagte er. „Ich wusste, dass ich mich darauf verlassen kann, dass ihr meinen besonderen Abend nicht vergesst."

Die Mumie trat vor, ihre Bandagen raschelten, als sie sich bewegte. „Ich habe dir ein besonderes Geschenk mitgebracht", sagte sie und hielt eine kleine, verpackte Schachtel hin.

Dracula nahm das Geschenk entgegen und packte es langsam aus, seine Augen weiteten sich, als er sah, was darin war. Es war ein neuer Umhang, aus feinster Seide gefertigt und mit Silberfaden bestickt.

the guests cried out in unison, their voices echoing through the room.

Dracula grinned widely, his fangs glinting in the dim light. "Thank you, my friends," he said. "I knew I could count on you to remember my special night."

The Mummy stepped forward, his bandages rustling as he spoke. "I have brought you a special gift," he said, holding out a small, wrapped package.

Dracula took the package and unwrapped it slowly, his eyes widening as he saw what was inside. It was a new cape, made from the finest silk and embroidered with silver thread.

„Mein Gott", sagte Dracula und strich mit den Fingern über den weichen Stoff. „Das ist wunderschön. Vielen Dank, mein lieber Freund."

Der Wolfsmensch trat als Nächstes vor, während er grollte. „Auch ich habe eine Überraschung für dich", sagte er und hielt eine kleine Flasche mit Flüssigkeit hoch. „Es ist ein Trank, der dich am Tag mächtig macht. Wir wissen, wie sehr du eine gute Herausforderung genießt."

Dracula nahm die Flasche und betrachtete sie genau. „Wie aufmerksam von euch", sagte er, seine Augen glänzten vor Aufregung. „Ich kann es kaum erwarten, es auszuprobieren."

Der unsichtbare Mann

"My goodness," Dracula said, running his fingers over the soft fabric. "This is absolutely beautiful. Thank you, my dear friend."

The Wolf Man stepped forward next, growling as he spoke. "I also have a surprise for you," he said, holding out a small bottle of liquid. "It's a potion that will make you powerful by daylight. We know how much you enjoy a good challenge."

Dracula took the bottle and examined it closely. "How thoughtful of you," he said, his eyes shining with excitement. "I can't wait to try it out."

The Invisible Man chuckled softly. "And I have

lachte leise. „Und ich habe auch eine Überraschung", sagte er und zeigte eine kleine, schwarze Katze. „Das ist Shadow – eine magische Katze, die dir hilft, ein Spiegelbild zu haben. Wir dachten, du könntest sie nützlich finden."

Dracula nahm die Katze und hielt sie fest, streichelte ihr glattes Fell. „Danke", sagte er mit Dankbarkeit in der Stimme. „Ihr wisst immer genau, was ich brauche. Trinkt aus, meine Freunde", sagte Dracula und lachte. „Heute Nacht werden wir uns festlich erfreuen." Mit diesen Worten wandte er sich an Sam, der auf dem Fass stand. „Lasst uns beginnen", sagte er und sein Gesicht erstrahlte in einem bösen Grinsen. Die Gäste kamen näher, ihre leeren Gläser ausgestreckt.

a surprise too," he said and showed a small, black cat. "This is Shadow—he's a magical cat that can help you to have a reflection in mirror. We thought you might find him useful."

Dracula took the cat and held it close, stroking its sleek fur. "Thank you," he said, his voice filled with gratitude. "You always know just what I need. Drink up, my friends," Dracula said with a chuckle. "Tonight, we shall feast." With these words he turned to Sam who stood on the barrel. "Let's start," he said, a wicked grin on his face. The guests came closer to them, their empty glasses held out.

Gerade als die Gäste sich in Bewegung setzen wollten, knarrte die Tür zum Saal auf. Tim trat herein und hielt die Puppe Manah in seiner Hand. Frau Smith, seine Lehrerin, folgte ihm dicht dahinter.

„Was passiert hier?" forderte Tim und betrachtete die Szene mit einer Mischung aus Verwirrung und Entsetzen.

Dracula drehte sich um, seine Augen glänzten vor Aufregung. „Ah, Tim", sagte er und grinste böse. „Willkommen auf unserer kleinen Party. Bist du dabei?"

Tim schüttelte energisch den Kopf. „Auf keinen Fall. Was tust du Sam an?"

Just as the guests were making their move, the door to the hall creaked open. Tim stepped inside, holding the doll Manah in his hand. Mrs. Smith, his teacher, followed closely behind him.

"What is going on here?" Tim demanded, eyeing the scene with a mixture of confusion and horror.

Dracula turned to face him, his eyes gleaming with excitement. "Ah, Tim," he said, grinning wickedly. "Welcome to our little party. Won't you join us?"

Tim shook his head firmly. "No way. What are you doing to Sam?"

Dracula lachte. „Oh, mach dir keine Sorgen um ihn. Wir haben nur ein bisschen Spaß."

Aber Tim war nicht überzeugt. Er trat einen Schritt vor, die Puppe vor sich ausgestreckt. „Du musst das jetzt sofort beenden", sagte er bestimmt. „Manah hier hat die Kraft, Menschen zu beschützen. Wenn du diesen Jungen nicht freilässt, wirst du es bereuen."

Tim trat vor, Manah auf Armeslänge haltend. Als er der Gruppe näher kam, konnte er spüren, wie ihre Angst wuchs. Aber er wusste, dass er ruhig bleiben musste, wenn er erfolgreich sein wollte.

Langsam streckte er die

Dracula laughed. "Oh, don't worry about him. We're just having a bit of fun."

But Tim was not convinced. He took a step forward, holding the doll out in front of him. "You need to stop this right now," he said firmly. "Manah here has the power to protect people. If you don't let that boy go, you're going to regret it."

Tim stepped forward, keeping Manah at arm's length. As he drew closer to the group, he could feel their fear growing. But he knew he had to remain calm if he wanted to succeed.

Slowly, he moved the

Arme der Puppe ausgestreckt in Richtung der Gäste. Zuerst geschah nichts - aber dann, langsam aber sicher, begannen Manahs Hände, länger und länger zu werden.

Die Gäste starrten entsetzt, erstarrt vor Schreck, als sie die Puppe näher kommen sahen. Dracula selbst trat einen Schritt zurück, seine Augen weiteten sich überrascht. Manahs Hände dehnten sich weiter und wurden immer länger. Die Gäste um Sam herum waren plötzlich erstarrt, als Manah sie mit seinen langen Händen berührte.

Dracula trat vor, seine Augen vor Wut zusammengekniffen. "Was soll das bedeuten?" verlangte er zu wissen, seine Stimme erhob sich über das

doll's arms outstretched towards the guests. At first, nothing happened—but then, slowly but surely, Manah's hands began to grow longer and longer.

The guests gasped in horror, frozen in place as they watched the doll approach. Dracula himself took a step back, his eyes widening in surprise. Manah's hands continued to stretch and elongate. The guests around Sam were suddenly frozen in place as Manah touched them with his long hands.

Dracula stepped forward, his eyes narrowed with anger. "What is the meaning of this?" he demanded, his voice rising

Flüstern der anderen Gäste.

Tim trat vor, Manah fest in seiner Hand haltend.

"Manah ist ein Beschüt-zer", sagte er bestimmt. "Er wird nicht zulassen, dass jemand Sam oder eine andere unschuldige Person verletzt."

Dracula schaute Tim an, dann Manah, dann wieder Tim. "Ich verstehe", sagte er langsam, mit einem Hauch von Bewunderung in seiner Stimme. "Gut gemacht, Tim. Du hast großen Mut in Gefahr gezeigt", fuhr Dracula fort. "Ich muss mich für mein Verhalten entschuldigen", sagte er. "Ich wollte Sam keinen Schaden zufügen. Ich wollte nur, dass er auf dem Fass tanzt, bevor es geöffnet wird, wie es unsere alte

above the hushed whispers of the other guests.

Tim stepped forward, holding Manah tightly in his hand.

"Manah is a protector," he said firmly. "He won't let anyone hurt Sam or any other innocent person."

Dracula looked at Tim, then at Manah, then back at Tim again. "I see," he said slowly, a hint of admiration in his voice. "Well done, Tim. You have shown great courage in the face of danger," Dracula continued. "I must apologize for my behavior," he said. "I meant no harm to Sam. I only wanted him to dance on the barrel with cyder before opening it, as is

rumänische Tradition ist."

Er wandte sich an seine Gäste, die immer noch erstarrt waren. "Lasst sie frei, Manah, bitte", sagte er sanft. Nachdem er das gesagt hatte, deutete Dracula den Musikern an und begann zu einer schönen rumänischen Musik rumänische Polka zu tanzen. Er zeigte, wie schön dieser Tanz war. Manahs Hände zogen sich langsam zurück und die Gäste konnten sich wieder bewegen. Sie schauten verwirrt umher, unsicher darüber, was gerade geschehen war.

Tim schaute Dracula an, dann Sam, der immer noch oben auf dem Fass stand. "Nun", sagte er mit einem Lächeln. "Warum tanzen wir nicht alle zusammen? Es scheint Spaß zu machen."

our old Romanian tradition."

He turned to his guests, who were still frozen in place. "Release them, Manah, please," he said softly. After saying that, Dracula gestured to musicians and began to dance Romanian polka to beautiful Romanian music. He showed how beautiful that dance was. Manah's hands slowly retracted, and the guests were once again able to move. They looked around confused, unsure of what had just happened.

Tim looked at Dracula, then at Sam, who was still standing at the top of the barrel. "Well," he said with a smile. "Why don't we all dance together? It sounds like fun."

Und so begannen zum Vergnügen aller im Saal Tim, Sam und alle Gäste, eine lebhafte rumänische Polka zu tanzen. Die Musik schwoll an, das Fass mit Cider wurde geöffnet und alle beteiligten sich an der Feier von Draculas Geburtsnacht.

Mit fortschreitender Nacht verabschiedeten sich Sam, Tim und Frau Smith und verließen den großen Saal. Sie fühlten sich sowohl erleichtert als auch glücklich, in Dracula einen neuen Freund gefunden zu haben.

And so, to the pleasure of everyone in the hall, Tim, Sam, and all guests began to dance a lively Romanian polka around the room. The music swelled, the barrel of cyder was opened, and everyone joined in the celebration of Dracula's birthnight.

As the night wore on, Sam, Tim and Mrs. Smith said their goodbyes and left the grand hall, feeling both relieved and happy to have made a new friend in Dracula.

¿?

Was wurde von Dracula und seinen Gästen gefeiert?

Warum hatte Sam Angst?

Wer waren die Gäste, die Dracula Geschenke gemacht

What was the occasion being celebrated by Dracula and his guests?

Why was Sam afraid?

Who were the guests

haben, und welche Geschenke haben Sie gemacht?

Was ist passiert, als Tim den Raum betreten hat, und wie hat er die Puppe Manah benutzt?

Wie reagierte Dracula auf Tims Eingreifen, und wofür entschuldigte er sich?

Was hat Dracula nach der Entschuldigung getan?

who gave gifts to Dracula, and what was the nature of their gifts?

What happened when Tim entered the room, and how did he use the doll Manah?

How did Dracula react to Tim's intervention, and what did he apologize for?

What did Dracula do after apologizing?

Kapitel 9

Eine schwarze Schachtel

A Black Box

Am nächsten Tag machten sich Sam, Tim und die anderen Kinder auf den Weg aus Draculas Schloss und fühlten sich immer noch etwas beunruhigt von ihrer Übernachtung. Als sie das Schloss verließen, verabschiedete sich Graf Dracula von ihnen.

The next day Sam, Tim and the other children made their way out of Dracula's castle, still feeling a little spooked from their one-night stay. As they made their way out of the castle, Count Dracula was seeing them off.

"Vielen Dank für Ihre Gastfreundschaft, Graf Dracula. Wir hatten eine beängstigende, aber unvergessliche Zeit", sagte Frau Smith lächelnd.

"Thank you for your hospitality, Count Dracula. We had a scary, but memorable time," Mrs. Smith said, smiling.

"Es war mir ein Vergnügen. Bitte kommen Sie bald wieder zu Besuch", antwortete Dracula

"It was my pleasure. Please come back and visit again soon," Dracula replied

mit einer Verbeugung.

Während die Gruppe ihre Taschen in den Bus lud, steckte Dracula unbemerkt eine kleine schwarze Schachtel in Frau Smiths Tasche.

Nach einigen Minuten stiegen die Kinder und die Lehrerin in den Bus und der Bus fuhr zum Flughafen. Als sie das Schloss verließen, verabschiedete sich Tim von den sanften Hügeln und dichten Wäldern, die das Schloss umgaben.

Später im Flugzeug nach New York scrollte Sam durch sein Handy, als er zufällig auf ein Video stieß, das er versehentlich aufgenommen hatte. Es war eine Szene vom Eingang des Schlosses, wo Dracula die

with a bow.

As the group was loading their bags onto the bus, Dracula slipped a little black box into Mrs. Smith's bag without her noticing.

In several minutes the children and the teacher got on the bus and the bus started for the airport. When they were leaving the castle, Tim said goodbye to the rolling hills and dense forests that surrounded the castle.

Later in the plane to New York, Sam was scrolling through his phone when he stumbled upon a video he accidentally recorded. It was a scene from the castle's entrance where Dracu-

kleine schwarze Schachtel in Frau Smiths Tasche steckte.

"Hey Tim, schau dir das an", flüsterte Sam und zeigte das Video Tim.

"Wow, denkst du, Dracula hat etwas in Frau Smiths Tasche gesteckt?", fragte Tim.

"Sieht ganz danach aus", antwortete Sam.

Die beiden Jungen konnten nicht aufhören, über die kleine schwarze Schachtel und deren Inhalt nachzudenken. Sobald sie in New York gelandet waren, erzählten sie Frau Smith von dem Vorfall.

" Frau Smith, wir glauben, dass Dracula etwas in Ihre Tasche gesteckt hat. Schauen Sie sich dieses Video an", sagte Sam und zeigte ihr die Aufnahme.

la slipped the little black box into Mrs. Smith's bag.

"Hey Tim, look at this," Sam whispered as he showed the video to Tim.

"Whoa, do you think Dracula put something in Mrs. Smith's bag?" Tim asked.

"It sure looks like it," Sam replied.

The two boys couldn't stop thinking about the little black box and what could be inside it. As soon as they landed in New York, they told Mrs. Smith about the incident.

"Mrs. Smith, we think Dracula put something in your bag. Look at this video," Sam said, showing her the recording.

Frau Smith sah das Video mit einem verwirrten Ausdruck im Gesicht. "Hmm, es sieht so aus, als hätte er das getan. Aber warum würde er das tun?", fragte sie sich.

"Ich weiß es nicht; vielleicht ist es eine alte rumänische Tradition, Geschenke auf diese Weise zu geben", schlug Sam vor.

Frau Smith nickte. "Das kann sein. Lasst mich meine Tasche überprüfen."

Als sie jedoch den Wartebereich des Flughafens erreichten und Frau Smith in ihre Tasche schaute, war die kleine schwarze Schachtel nirgendwo zu finden.

"Ich kann die Schachtel nicht finden. Vielleicht ist sie während des Fluges herausgefallen", sagte Frau Smith enttäuscht.

Mrs. Smith watched the video with a puzzled expression on her face. "Hmm, it looks like he did. But why would he do that?" she wondered.

"I don't know; maybe it's an old Romanian tradition to give presents in such a way," Sam suggested.

Mrs. Smith nodded. "That could be it. Let me check my bag."

However, when they reached the waiting room of the airport and Mrs. Smith looked in her bag, the little black box was nowhere to be found.

"I can't find the box. Maybe it fell out during the flight," Mrs. Smith said, sounding disappointed.

Gleichzeitig erklang eine Durchsage.

"Achtung, alle Passagiere, bitte verlassen Sie sofort den Sektor B des Flughafens. Es breitet sich ein schwarzer Nebel im Bereich aus."

Frau Smith und die Kinder verließen schnell den Flughafen und fuhren nach Hause. Sie konnten nicht anders, als sich über die kleine schwarze Schachtel und deren Inhalt zu wundern.

Der Abend war aufregend, aber Tim konnte das Gefühl nicht abschütteln, dass etwas nicht stimmte. Er beschloss, etwas über rumänische Traditionen zu recherchieren, um herauszufinden, ob es tatsächlich üblich war, Geschenke zu geben, ohne dass die Empfänger davon

At the same time, an announcement sounded.

"Attention all passengers, please vacate sector B of the airport immediately. There is a black fog spreading through the area."

Mrs. Smith and the kids quickly left the airport and drove to their homes. They couldn't help but wonder about the little black box and what it might have contained.

The evening was exciting, but Tim couldn't shake off the feeling that something wasn't right. He decided to do some research on Romanian traditions to see if giving gifts to someone without them knowing was really a thing. After

wussten. Nach stundenlanger Suche fand er eine alte Legende über einen geheimnisvollen Nebel, der in einigen Regionen Rumäniens auftauchte, wenn eine dunkle Macht am Werk war. Es hieß, dass der schwarze Nebel eine Warnung an diejenigen war, die es wagten, in die unbekannten tiefen Wälder um Graf Draculas Schloss einzudringen. Tim konnte nicht glauben, was er las.

War es möglich, dass Dracula einen Fluch auf die Schachtel gelegt hatte, die er in Frau Smiths Tasche gesteckt hatte?

Als die Nacht über New York hereinbrach, leuchteten die Sterne wie Diamanten am Himmel. Tim schlief in seinem Bett. Inzwischen stand Manah

hours of searching, he found an old legend about a mysterious fog that would appear in some regions of Romania whenever a dark force was at work. It was said that the black fog was a warning to those who dared to intrude into the unknown deep forests around Count Dracula's castle. Tim couldn't believe what he was reading.

Was it possible that Dracula had put a curse on the box that he put into Mrs. Smith's bag?

As the night settled over New York, the stars shone like diamonds in the sky. Tim was asleep in his bed. Meanwhile, on the

auf dem Fensterbrett.

Er hielt in seiner Hand einen kleinen roten Stein, den er Dracula in jener Nacht im Schloss abgenommen hatte.

Der Stein in Form eines Tropfens glitzerte im Mondlicht. Manah überwachte die Straßen unten, wachsam auf Anzeichen von Gefahr. Er wusste, dass die Stadt ein gefährlicher Ort sein konnte, besonders nachts, und er war entschlossen, Tim in Sicherheit zu halten. Und obwohl die Nacht lang und dunkel war, wusste er, dass er nicht ruhen würde, bis die Sonne aufging und Tim wieder sicher war.

(Fortsetzung folgt...)

windowsill, Manah stood guard.

In his hand, Manah held a small, red stone that he took away from Dracula that night in the castle.

The stone in the shape of a drop glittered in the moonlight. Manah scanned the streets below, alert for any signs of danger. He knew that the city could be a dangerous place, especially at night, and he was determined to keep Tim safe. And though the night was long and dark, he knew that he would not rest until the sun rose and Tim was safe once more.

(to be continued ...)

¿?

Wie fühlten sich die Kinder, als sie das Schloss verließen?

How did the children feel as they left the castle?

Was entdeckten Sam und Tim im Flugzeug nach New York?

What did Sam and Tim discover on the plane to New York?

Hat Frau Smith die kleine schwarze Schachtel in ihrer Tasche gefunden?

Did Mrs. Smith find the little black box in her bag?

Was ist am Flughafen passiert, während sie nach der Schachtel gesucht haben?

What happened at the airport while they were looking for the box?

Welche Legende hat Tim über die tiefen Wälder um Graf Draculas Schloss gefunden?

What legend did Tim find about deep forests around Count Dracula's castle?

Recommended reading

First German Reader for Beginners

(Volume 1) Bilingual for Speakers of English Beginner Elementary (A1 A2)

The method utilizes the natural human ability to remember words used in texts repeatedly and systematically. With the translation on the same page, you can effortlessly learn what any unfamiliar words mean. You can quickly pick up new vocabulary and phrases that are used over and over in the book. As you read the book, your brain begins to remember words and phrases simply because you are exposed to them several times.

First German Reader (Volume 2)

Bilingual for Speakers of English

Elementary (A2)

This book is Volume 2 of First German Reader for Beginners. The method utilizes the natural human ability to remember words used in texts repeatedly and systematically. The audio tracks and samples are available inclusive online.

First German Reader (Volume 3)

Bilingual for Speakers of English

Elementary (A2)

This book is Volume 3 of First German Reader for Beginners. The method utilizes the natural human ability to remember words used in texts repeatedly and systematically. The audio tracks and samples are available inclusive on www.audiolego.com/Book/German-3

First German Reader for Beginners
Bilingual for Children and Parents
Beginner (A1)

The book contains a beginner's course for children with parallel German-English translation. The method utilizes the natural human ability to remember words used in texts repeatedly and systematically. The audio tracks and a sample are available inclusive online.

First German Reader for Students
Bilingual for Speakers of English
Beginner Elementary (A1 A2)

Each chapter is filled with words that are organized by topic, then used in a story in German. Questions and answers rephrase information and text is repeated in English to aid comprehension. The quick and easy-to-use format organizes many of life's situations from knowing your way around the house, studying at university, or getting a job. The audio tracks and samples are available inclusive online.

First German Reader for Cooking
Bilingual for Speakers of English
Beginner Elementary (A1 A2)

When learning a language, familiarity in the subject helps connect one language to another. The First German Reader for Cooking provides the words and phrases in both English and German. It might make you hungry or it might help German language learners like you improve their understanding in a familiar setting of the kitchen. The audio tracks and samples are available inclusive on www.audiolego.com/Book/German-9

First German Reader for Business

Bilingual for Speakers of English Beginner Elementary (A1 A2)

The First German Reader for Business is a resource that guides conversational bilinguals with the German vocabulary, phrases, and questions that are relevant to many situations in the workplace. It is the book to help the businessperson take their German language knowledge to the professional level.

First German Medical Reader for Health Professions and Nursing

Bilingual for Speakers of English Beginner Elementary (A1 A2)

First German Medical Reader will give you the words and phrases necessary for helping patients making appointments, informing them of their diagnosis, and their treatment options. Medical specialties range from ENT to dentistry. The method utilizes the natural human ability to remember words used in texts repeatedly and systematically.

First German Reader for the Family

Bilingual for Speakers of English Beginner Elementary (A1 A2)

How do you ask in a clear and precise way about relatives of your friends? How do you answer questions about your family and other beloved ones? Ask and answer questions about situations at home, on your way to school or university, at work, in hospital etc. Through this method, a person will be able to enhance his or her ability to remember the words that has been incorporated

into consequent sentences. The audio tracks and samples are available inclusive on www.audiolego.com/Book/German-15

Thomas's Fears and Hopes
Short Stories in Plain Spoken German
Bilingual for speakers of English
Pre-intermediate (B1)

Thomas had returned home to Georgia for his father's funeral. He became informed that he would receive the entire estate as he was the only child. Then a few events happened that scared him. The audio tracks are available inclusive online.

First German Reader for Tourists
Bilingual for Speakers of English
Beginner (A1)

If you would like to travel and learn German at A1 level, this book is the best choice. Unlike a phrasebook, it is composed with the thought of systematic learning approach. The audio tracks and samples are available inclusive on www.audiolego.com/Book/German-14

Learn German Language Through Dialogue
Bilingual for Speakers of English
Beginner Elementary (A1 A2)

The textbook gives you a lot of examples on how questions in German should be formed. It is easy to see the difference between German and English using parallel translation. Common questions and answers used in everyday situations are explained simply enough even for beginners. Some sayings

and jokes make it engaging despite four cases that make German a little difficult for some students. The audio tracks and samples are available inclusive on www.audiolego.com/Book/German-5

Fremde Wasser

Intermediate German Reader

Parallel translation

Being a co-founder of a two-men business has its pros and cons. The cold waters of self-employment do not fit everyone. The audio tracks are available inclusive on www.audiolego.com/Book/German-7

Schatten der Vergangenheit

Intermediate level

Bilingual for Speakers of English

Forensic science was one of Damien Morin's passions. However, the first real crime that he investigated led him to his own past. The audio tracks are available inclusive online.

Made in the USA
Coppell, TX
05 March 2025

46719077R00046